delish

Amazing Recipes FOR Picky Eaters

GENIUS IDEAS
FOR PEOPLE WHO LIKE ALMOST NOTHING

FROM THE EDITORS OF delish

EDITORIAL DIRECTOR Joanna Saltz

FOOD DIRECTOR Lauren Miyashiro

DIRECTOR OF CONTENT OPERATIONS
Lindsey Ramsey

ART DIRECTOR Alexandra Folino

DESIGNER Banna Tesfay

SENIOR FOOD EDITOR Lena Abraham

ASSISTANT FOOD EDITOR Makinze Gore

SENIOR FOOD PRODUCER June (Jiuxing) Xie

TEST KITCHEN ASSISTANT Justin Sullivan

Hearst Product Studio

VP, CONSUMER PRODUCTS Sheel Shah

SENIOR EDITOR Missy Steinberg

ASSOCIATE EDITOR Patricia Reyes

**CHIEF CONTENT OFFICER,
HEARST MAGAZINES** Kate Lewis

**SVP, CHIEF REVENUE OFFICER,
HEARST DIGITAL MEDIA** Todd Haskell

VP, EXECUTIVE DIRECTOR, SALES Sue Katzen

SALES DIRECTORS Corianne Carroll,
Tracy Leiken Chafetz, Kimberly Parrilla

MARKETING DIRECTOR Dina Gallo

MARKETING MANAGER Nicole Guba

**PUBLISHED BY HEARST COMMUNICATIONS, INC.
PRESIDENT & CHIEF EXECUTIVE OFFICER**
Steven R. Swartz

CHAIRMAN William R. Hearst III

EXECUTIVE VICE CHAIRMAN Frank A. Bennack, Jr.

SECRETARY Catherine A. Bostron

TREASURER Carlton Charles

HEARST MAGAZINES DIVISION

**ACTING PRESIDENT, HEARST MAGAZINES
GROUP AND TREASURER** Debi Chirichella

**PRESIDENT, MARKETING
AND PUBLISHING DIRECTOR** Michael Clinton

PUBLISHING CONSULTANTS Gilbert C. Maurer,
Mark F. Miller

Cover Photography by Erik Bernstein
Back Cover Photography by Suzanne Clements
Interior Photography by Erik Bernstein, Ethan Calabrese, Suzanne Clements, Parker Feierbach, Judy Kim, Erika Lapresto, Lucy Schaffer, and Kat Wirsing
Cover Hand Lettering by Banna Tesfay

Library of Congress Cataloging–in–Publication Data is on file with the publisher.

978-1-950099-76-4   2 4 6 8 10 9 7 5 3 1 paperback

HEARST

IT DOESN'T MATTER WHO THE PICKY EATER IS.

If you're a parent, you know the drill. One day your child is an adventurous, trusting baby who eats everything you put on their tray. Then, in what seems like the blink of an eye, you're faced with a stubborn (albeit cute) little monster who's resistant to anything new. It's a frustrating and disappointing transition. One in which the temptation to just give up, and give them a bowl of mac & cheese or chicken fingers or literally whatever the heck they want, is all too real.

OR, maybe you're not a parent, and you're holding this book because all your friends say you eat like a 5-year-old. You're the date who always suggests pizza or the guest at the wedding who sticks to the bread bowl or the coworker stressing way too much over the menu at a client dinner.

Everyone is, or was at some point in their life, picky. To grow out of it takes persistence, patience, creativity, and, in our opinion, delicious food. Sometimes this means you disguise cauliflower as pizza crust (p. 35). Other times it involves slathering roast salmon with the familiar taste of honey mustard (p. 72). It's not about trickery—it's an introduction to newness in a non-overwhelming, nonjudgmental way.

For this guide, we didn't just collect our best "kid-friendly" meals. We carefully selected breakfasts, lunches, dinners, and snacks that everyone at the table will love. Each recipe is a gateway to more. More ingredients, textures, flavors, and ideas. More vegetables. More deliciousness and fun.

XO, JO SALTZ

CONTENTS

80

CHAPTER 3

DINNER

120

CHAPTER 4

VEGGIES

CHAPTER 5

SNACKS

DO'S & DON'TS
WHEN DEALING WITH PICKY EATERS
—REGARDLESS OF AGE

1 Do start with something familiar.

New foods feel less off-putting when they come in the form of an old, familiar friend. Like your BFF, chicken primavera. It's impossible not to welcome squash or zucchini into your life when it's covered in mozzarella, Parm, and roasted tomatoes (like it is on p. 76). Your favorites + a little something new = true love, we promise.

2 Don't be a short-order cook.

Catering to the pickiness sends the message that selective eating habits are acceptable. And if you're an adult, this kind of cooking just boxes you in. Rather than become a short order cook, try to give options with a meal so there's always some variety to choose from. Whenever you can, serve garnishes for pasta and toppings for, say, fajitas and breakfast tacos, on the table for people to personalize their plate.

3 Do keep trying.

If you totally hated a food the first time it was served, that doesn't mean that ingredient is ruled out forever. In fact, research suggests it can take a person 11 tries to develop a taste for a new food.

4 Don't knock a dish based on its ingredients.

You may think you hate cauliflower. Heck, you might actually, truly hate cauliflower. But when you blend it with other less-hated ingredients, the end result isn't even technically cauliflower anymore. It becomes something entirely new. Which is the magic of really good cooking and what you are going to do with this book.

5 **Do have fun.**

Feeding a picky eater takes a lot of effort and patience—even if that picky eater is you! But the more inspired and playful your menu is, the more enjoyable it'll be for everyone. Go ahead and throw potato chips into your eggs (p. 10) or call Tuesday's dinner "Hamburger Soup" (p. 95). When you take meal time a little less seriously, there's less pressure.

6 **Don't force it.**

Never count bites or have a set expectation for how much of a food a person should eat. This can create an unhealthy dynamic with food and make it hard for someone to trust when they're full.

7 **Do prioritize quality groceries.**

It is possible that the last time you tried apples, you simply had one that was underripe, overripe, out of season, or just plain bad. And therefore it is also possible that you might not dislike all apples, just that unfortunate one. Visit your local farmers' market and sample something in-season. Quality ingredients taste better.

8 **Don't forget to do it your way.**

If that means slathering everything in ranch, so be it. Food is meant to be fun. Put your personal twist on everything you make and know that there are no rules. Except maybe to always add extra cheese.

CHAPTER 1

BREAKFAST

POTATO CHIP FRITTATA

SERVES 4 • TOTAL TIME: 55 MIN

We've met no one who's able to resist sour cream and onion potato chips (if you can, let us in on your superpower), and when they get soaked in eggy custard something magical happens. They soften just enough to mimic thinly sliced potatoes in Tortilla Española, one of Spain's most beloved dishes.

2 tablespoons extra-virgin olive oil

½ medium yellow onion, minced

8 large eggs

¼ cup sour cream, plus more for garnish

1½ cups sour cream & onion chips, plus more for garnish

2 tablespoons freshly chopped chives, plus more for garnish

Kosher salt

Freshly ground black pepper

1. Preheat oven to 375° and heat oil in a medium skillet over medium heat. Add onion and cook, stirring occasionally, until they are golden and caramelized, 20 to 25 minutes.

2. Meanwhile, combine eggs and sour cream in a large bowl and whisk to combine. Add chips and chives, and stir to combine. Let sit 10 minutes, then season with salt and pepper.

3. When onions are caramelized, pour egg mixture into skillet and stir to evenly distribute potato chips.

4. Transfer skillet to oven and bake until eggs are just set, 10 to 12 minutes.

5. Let cool 5 minutes, then garnish with sour cream, more chips, and more chives before serving.

PRO TIP!

Grate the cauliflower
directly into the
baking dish.

LOADED CAULIFLOWER BREAKFAST BAKE

SERVES 6 • TOTAL TIME: 1 HR 15 MIN

"I miss the hash browns," said no one ever after devouring this insanely flavorful bacon–cheddar casserole.

---

1 large head cauliflower

8 slices bacon, chopped

10 large eggs

1 cup whole milk

2 cloves garlic, minced

2 teaspoons paprika

Kosher salt

Freshly ground black pepper

2 cups shredded cheddar

2 green onions, thinly sliced, plus more for garnish (optional)

Hot sauce, for serving

1. Preheat oven to 350°. Grate cauliflower head on a box grater and transfer to a large baking dish.

2. In a large skillet over medium heat, cook bacon until crispy, 8 minutes. Transfer to a paper towel–lined plate to drain fat.

3. In a large bowl, whisk together eggs, milk, garlic, and paprika. Season with salt and pepper.

4. Top cauliflower with cheddar, cooked bacon, and green onions, and pour over egg mixture on top.

5. Bake until eggs are set and top is golden, 35 to 40 minutes.

6. Garnish with hot sauce and more green onions, if using, before serving.

BEST-EVER PARFAIT

SERVES 2 • TOTAL TIME: 25 MIN

When blueberries on their own won't do the trick, blueberry compote always will. Sure, the word sounds fancy, but don't fret—simmering fruit (fresh or frozen!), water, and sugar in a saucepan is one easy technique you'll thank us for later.

---

2 cups fresh or frozen blueberries

¼ cup water

¼ cup granulated sugar

Pinch kosher salt

2 teaspoons freshly grated lemon zest

1⅓ cups yogurt, divided

½ cup granola, divided

1. To make compote: Combine blueberries, water, sugar, and salt in a small saucepan. Heat over medium heat until blueberries begin to burst and a spoon or spatula leaves a clear path on the bottom of your pot, 8 to 10 minutes. Remove from heat, stir in lemon zest, and let cool 10 minutes.

2. Build your parfaits: Add ⅓ cup yogurt to the bottom of two glasses. Top each with ¼ of the blueberry mixture, ¼ cup of granola, another ⅓ cup of yogurt, and the remaining blueberry compote.

HEALTHY PUMPKIN MUFFINS

MAKES 15 · TOTAL TIME: 50 MIN

We can't decide if it's the pumpkin pie spice, the honey, or the pecans, but these are the muffins that will *finally* turn your pumpkin onto pumpkin.

1 cup all-purpose flour

½ cup whole wheat flour

1 teaspoon baking powder

½ teaspoon baking soda

½ teaspoon kosher salt

2 teaspoons pumpkin pie spice

1 cup canned pumpkin

½ cup honey

2 large eggs

6 tablespoons butter, melted and cooled

¼ cup Greek yogurt

1 cup toasted and chopped pecans

2 tablespoons Demerara sugar

1. Preheat oven to 325° and line muffin tin with liners.

2. In a large bowl, whisk together flours, baking powder, baking soda, salt, and pumpkin pie spice. Add pumpkin, honey, eggs, butter, and yogurt, and mix until combined. Fold in ¾ cup pecans.

3. Divide batter into muffin liners, then top with remaining pecans and Demerara sugar. Bake until muffins are golden brown and a toothpick comes out clean, about 30 minutes. Let muffins cool in pan, then serve.

TRIPLE BERRY SMOOTHIE

SERVES 2 • TOTAL TIME: 5 MIN

The fruit smoothie formula to memorize. We think strawberries, blackberries, and raspberries make the perfect trio, but change it up based on what fruit your picky eater loves most.

---

1 banana

1 cup frozen strawberries

1 cup frozen blackberries

1 cup frozen raspberries

1¼ cups almond milk

½ cup Greek yogurt

1. In a blender, combine all ingredients and blend until smooth.

2. Divide into two servings and top with more berries, if desired.

PRO TIP!

If you sub in tropical
fruit like pineapple or
mango, swap almond
for coconut milk.

BANANA ALMOND FLOUR PANCAKES

SERVES 2 · TOTAL TIME: 30 MIN

In our experience, picky eaters will chow down on anything that resembles a flapjack—so better sneak in the good stuff like bananas and almond flour. Totally gluten free, these get their wildly fluffy texture from whipped egg whites.

4 large eggs, separated

2 ripe bananas, mashed (about 1 cup)

1 cup almond flour

3 tablespoons coconut flour

1 teaspoon baking powder

¼ teaspoon ground cinnamon (optional)

Pinch kosher salt

Cooking spray

Butter, for serving

Maple syrup, for serving

Berries, for serving

1. In a large bowl, whisk together egg yolks, bananas, almond flour, coconut flour, baking powder, cinnamon (if using), and salt. In a separate large bowl using a hand or standing mixer, whip egg whites until stiff peaks form, 4 to 5 minutes.

2. Gently fold whipped egg whites into batter until evenly combined.

3. Grease a large nonstick pan with cooking spray and place over medium-low heat. Pour about ¼ cup pancake batter onto the pan, spreading it out evenly. Cook until both sides are lightly golden. Serve with butter, maple syrup, and berries.

CINNAMON ROLL BAKED OATMEAL

SERVES 10 • TOTAL TIME: 1 HR 15 MIN

When in doubt, turn it into a cinnamon roll. We're already suckers for baked oatmeal but spike it with cinnamon and add cream cheese icing and everyone will be obsessed.

FOR OATS

1 tablespoon butter, for pan

5 cups rolled oats

1⅓ cups toasted walnuts, roughly chopped, divided

1 tablespoon ground cinnamon

3 teaspoons baking powder

1 teaspoon kosher salt

4½ cups whole milk

½ cup heavy cream

½ cup maple syrup

2 large eggs, lightly beaten

2 teaspoons pure vanilla extract

FOR FROSTING

4 ounces cream cheese, softened

⅓ cup butter, softened

1 cup powdered sugar

2 tablespoons heavy cream

1. Preheat oven to 375° and butter a 9x13-inch baking dish. In a large bowl, stir together oats, walnuts, cinnamon, baking powder, and salt.

2. In another large bowl, whisk together milk, heavy cream, maple syrup, eggs, and vanilla. Pour dry ingredients into prepared pan, then pour wet ingredients over them. Stir to ensure there are no dry spots.

3. Bake 40 to 45 minutes, until top is golden and no liquid remains.

4. Meanwhile, make frosting: In a large bowl, combine butter and cream cheese and beat until light and fluffy. Add powdered sugar and beat until smooth. Gradually add heavy cream to loosen.

5. Let oatmeal cool, 10 minutes. Cut into squares and serve with a drizzle of frosting and a sprinkle of toasted walnuts.

PRO TIP!

Blueberries on the
will–not–eat list?
Sub in raspberries
or blackberries.

CLASSIC BLUEBERRY MUFFINS

MAKES 12 • TOTAL TIME: 45 MIN

Do yourself a favor: Always keep a batch of these super-easy (and super-delish) muffins in your freezer for the times when you *just can't*. They're the perfect healthy-ish treat for a lunchbox or playdate.

---

2 cups all-purpose flour

1 teaspoon baking powder

½ teaspoon baking soda

¼ teaspoon kosher salt

½ cup (1 stick) unsalted butter, softened

1 cup sugar, plus 1 tablespoon for sprinkling

2 large eggs

1 teaspoon pure vanilla extract

¾ cups Greek yogurt

1¾ cups fresh blueberries, divided

---

1. Preheat oven to 350° and line a muffin tin with muffin cups.

2. In a large bowl, whisk together flour, baking powder, baking soda, and salt. Set aside. Meanwhile, in another large bowl using a hand mixer, cream together butter and 1 cup sugar until light and fluffy. Add eggs and beat to incorporate, then mix in vanilla and Greek yogurt. In three additions, add dry ingredients, mixing on low speed until smooth. Gently fold in 1½ cups blueberries.

3. Scoop batter into muffin cups. Place remaining blueberries on top and sprinkle tops with sugar.

4. Bake muffins until a toothpick comes out clean, 25 to 28 minutes. Let muffins cool slightly in pan, then cool completely on rack.

BEST BREAKFAST TACOS

Hands down our favorite way to breakfast any day of the week. Simmering the potatoes in water for just a few minutes ensures you won't be stirring (and stirring) them over the stove.

1 large russet potato, peeled and diced into ½-inch pieces

Kosher salt

1 tablespoon extra-virgin olive oil, plus more as needed

4 ounces fresh chorizo sausage, casing removed if necessary

¼ small yellow onion, diced

Freshly ground black pepper

2 tablespoons butter

3 large eggs, beaten

4 medium flour tortillas

½ cup shredded cheddar

Hot sauce, for serving

2 green onions, thinly sliced, for serving

Sliced avocado, for serving (optional)

Pickled onions, for serving (optional)

1. Place potatoes in a large pot and cover with 1 inch of cold water. Season water with 1 teaspoon kosher salt and bring to a boil. Simmer until potatoes are tender, 3 to 5 minutes. Drain.

2. Meanwhile, in a large skillet over medium heat, heat olive oil. Add chorizo and onion. Cook, stirring occasionally, until chorizo is cooked through and onions are translucent, 6 to 8 minutes.

3. Move chorizo and onion to the edges of your skillet and add another tablespoon of oil if the skillet looks dry. Add drained potatoes to the center of the skillet and spread out in an even layer. Let cook undisturbed until undersides of potatoes begin to turn brown and crisp, 4 to 6 minutes. Stir potatoes into chorizo and turn off heat.

4. Make eggs: In a medium nonstick skillet, melt butter. Pour eggs into the pan and let set slightly, then reduce heat to medium-low. Drag the eggs with a spatula or wooden spoon to create curds. When the eggs are cooked to your liking, season with salt and pepper and remove from heat.

5. Build the tacos: Lightly toast each of your tortillas over an open flame or in a large dry skillet, then transfer to serving plates. Divide cheddar evenly between tortillas, then top with a scoop of chorizo and potatoes, and a scoop of eggs. Serve with your choice of garnishes—and don't forget the hot sauce!

PRO TIP!

If chorizo has too much kick, go for breakfast sausage or bacon instead.

BEST-EVER BELGIAN WAFFLES

SERVES 4 · TOTAL TIME: 15 MIN

Let's face it: No matter your age, waffles always win. These get their signature crispy-on-the-outside, fluffy-on-the-inside texture from beating egg whites. Thank the sour cream for the addictive tang.

---

2 cups all-purpose flour

1 tablespoon granulated sugar

1 teaspoon baking powder

½ teaspoon kosher salt

½ teaspoon baking soda

1 cup sour cream

1 cup milk

6 tablespoons butter, melted, plus more for waffle iron

3 large eggs, separated

1. In a large bowl, whisk together flour, sugar, baking powder, salt, and baking soda. In a separate bowl, whisk together sour cream, milk, butter, and egg yolks. Gently fold wet mixture into dry mixture.

2. In a large bowl, using a hand mixer (or in the bowl of a stand mixer), beat egg whites until stiff peaks form. Fold whipped egg whites into batter, being careful not to overmix. (A few fluffy streaks of whites are fine!)

3. Heat waffle iron according to manufacturer's instructions. When the iron is hot, brush grates with melted butter. Spoon about ⅓ cup of batter into waffle maker and cook until golden, about 5 minutes. Repeat with remaining batter.

CHAPTER 2

LUNCH

CHICKEN PESTO PANINI

SERVES 2 · TOTAL TIME: 40 MIN

Pssst, no panini press necessary. To achieve the coveted char, we use a grill pan and weigh down the sandwich with a heavy skillet (stacking two skillets also works). Have fun with your fillings— avocado, turkey, and Parmesan is another go-to combo—but always use sturdy, crusty bread like ciabatta or focaccia.

4 tablespoons extra-virgin olive oil, divided

2 boneless, skinless chicken breasts

1 teaspoon dried oregano

¼ teaspoon crushed red pepper flakes

Kosher salt

Freshly ground black pepper

2 ciabatta rolls

¼ cup pesto

1 tomato, thinly sliced

4 ounces fresh mozzarella, thinly sliced

1. In a large cast iron skillet over medium heat, heat 2 tablespoons oil. Season chicken with oregano, red pepper flakes, salt, and pepper. Add chicken to skillet and cook until golden and cooked through, 7 minutes per side. Remove from pan.

2. Build panini: Slice ciabatta rolls in half, then spread about ¼ of the pesto on bottom half of each roll. Top with tomato, chicken, and mozzarella. Spread remaining pesto on the top half of each roll.

3. Heat a grill pan with remaining 2 tablespoons oil and add one panini. Cook until bottom is golden and cheese is starting to melt, 5 minutes. Flip then place a heavy skillet on top of sandwich and press down to flatten panini. Cook until golden and cheese is completely melted, another 5 minutes. Repeat with remaining panini.

CAULIFLOWER PIZZA BITES

SERVES 6 • TOTAL TIME: 45 MIN

We've never met a vegetable topped with red sauce, melty mozzarella, and pepperoni that we didn't like. These bite–size pizzas not only ditch the gluten—they'll make you legitimately excited to eat cauliflower.

---

1 large head cauliflower

2 large eggs

1 cup shredded mozzarella, divided

¼ cup freshly grated Parmesan

3 tablespoons finely chopped fresh basil, divided

1½ teaspoons garlic powder

Kosher salt

Freshly ground black pepper

½ cup marinara

¼ cup mini pepperoni

1. Preheat oven to 400°. Grate cauliflower on the small side of a box grater to form fine crumbs. Transfer to a large bowl.

2. Add eggs, ⅓ cup mozzarella, Parmesan, 2 tablespoons basil, and garlic powder to bowl and season with salt and pepper. Form into small patties (they will be wet) and place on a greased baking sheet. Bake until golden, 20 minutes.

3. Top each cauliflower patty with a thin layer of marinara, a sprinkle of the remaining mozzarella, and mini pepperoni and bake until cheese melts and pepperoni crisps, 5 to 7 minutes more.

4. Garnish with remaining basil and serve.

SWEET BBQ LIME CHICKEN TACOS

SERVES 4 • TOTAL TIME: 50 MIN

We've been known to say that the kicked-up barbecue sauce on these breaded chicken tenders is dangerously delish. With a drizzle of ranch? Beyond. Don't say we didn't warn you.

- 2 pounds boneless, skinless chicken breasts, cut into 2-inch pieces
- 1 cup all-purpose flour
- 2 cups panko bread crumbs
- 3 large eggs
- Kosher salt
- Freshly ground black pepper
- 1 cup barbecue sauce
- ½ cup packed brown sugar
- Juice of 2 limes
- 1 teaspoon garlic powder
- 8 small flour tortillas
- ½ head green cabbage, shredded
- ¼ cup ranch dressing, for drizzling
- 2 tablespoons freshly chopped cilantro, for garnish

1. Preheat oven to 425° and line a large baking sheet with parchment. In a large resealable plastic bag, combine chicken and flour and shake until fully coated.

2. In one bowl, add bread crumbs. In another bowl, beat eggs. Dip chicken in eggs, then in panko until fully coated. Transfer to prepared baking sheet and season with salt and pepper.

3. Bake until golden and crispy, 23 to 25 minutes.

4. Meanwhile, in a small saucepan over low heat, warm barbecue sauce, brown sugar, lime juice, and garlic powder.

5. Coat baked chicken in sauce.

6. Serve chicken in tortillas with cabbage and drizzled with ranch. Garnish with cilantro.

MINI PEPPER PIZZAS

SERVES 4 • TOTAL TIME: 30 MIN

When pizza is the only thing that'll please, try serving it in bell peppers—the halves make tasty baking vessels for ingredients. Mini pepperoni look cuter on these, but regular ones totally work, too.

---

4 bell peppers, halved and cored

1 tablespoon extra-virgin olive oil

Kosher salt

Freshly ground black pepper

½ cup pizza sauce

2 cups shredded mozzarella

½ cup finely grated Parmesan

⅓ cup mini pepperoni

1 tablespoon chopped parsley

1. Preheat oven to 350°. On a sheet tray, drizzle peppers with olive oil and season with salt and pepper.

2. Spoon sauce onto each pepper half. Sprinkle with mozzarella and Parmesan and top with pepperoni. Bake for 10 to 15 minutes, until the peppers are crisp-tender and the cheese is melted.

3. Garnish with parsley before serving.

CHICKEN AVOCADO ROLL-UPS

Tortilla pinwheels: way more fun to eat than a sandwich and can work with pretty much whatever deli meat and veggies you have in your fridge. Just chop up everything into bite–size pieces, mix 'em up, spread onto your tortilla, and get ready to roll.

2 avocados, cubed

Juice of 1 lime

2 cups shredded chicken

1 bell pepper, seed and core removed, chopped

½ small red onion, chopped

½ cup shredded Monterey jack

½ cup shredded cheddar

2 tablespoons sour cream

2 tablespoons finely chopped chives

4 large flour tortillas

1. In a medium bowl, combine avocado and lime juice and mash until only small chunks of avocado remain. Add chicken, bell pepper, red onion, Monterey jack, cheddar, sour cream, and chives and stir until evenly combined.

2. Spread a thin layer of the chicken avocado mixture onto a large tortilla, leaving a small border around the edges. Roll the tortilla up tightly, then cut off the edges and slice into 1–inch rolls. Repeat with remaining ingredients.

3. Serve cold or at room temperature.

WORLD'S GREATEST HAM SANDWICH

MAKES 4 • TOTAL TIME: 15 MIN

You're probably thinking, "I don't need a ham sandwich recipe." But making your own herb mayo—by mixing in a few fresh herbs and some olive oil—will make this sandwich stand above the rest.

FOR THE HERB MAYO

1 cup mayonnaise

2 tablespoons freshly chopped parsley

2 teaspoons freshly chopped thyme

1 tablespoon extra-virgin olive oil

2 cloves garlic, minced

FOR THE SANDWICH

8 slices crusty bread, such as sourdough or ciabatta

¼ cup Dijon mustard

12 slices deli ham

8 slices provolone

1 bunch arugula

1 tomato, thinly sliced

½ red onion, thinly sliced

1. In a medium bowl whisk together mayonnaise, parsley, thyme, oil, and garlic.

2. Spread 2 tablespoons herb mayo on 4 slices of bread. Spread 1 tablespoon mustard on the other 4 slices of bread. Top each mayo slice of bread with 3 slices of ham, 2 slices of provolone, arugula, a couple slices of tomato, and red onion. Top with remaining bread slices, mustard side down.

CHICKEN PASTA SALAD

SERVES 8 • TOTAL TIME: 30 MIN

A pasta salad to end all others. It's got the perfect ratio of mix-ins: meaty (chicken, bacon), fresh (baby spinach and tomatoes), and creamy (feta). Bonus: Leftovers of this taste even better.

FOR SALAD

1 pound fusilli pasta

2 boneless, skinless chicken breasts (about 1 pound)

1 teaspoon garlic powder

Kosher salt

Freshly ground black pepper

1 tablespoon extra-virgin olive oil

4 slices bacon, cooked and crumbled

2 cups halved grape tomatoes

2 cups spinach, packed

½ cup crumbled feta

¼ red onion, thinly sliced

2 tablespoons freshly chopped dill

FOR DRESSING

¼ cup extra-virgin olive oil

3 tablespoons red wine vinegar

½ teaspoon Italian seasoning

1 clove garlic, minced

1 tablespoon Dijon mustard

1. In a large pot of salted boiling water, cook fusilli according to package directions until al dente. Drain and transfer to large bowl.

2. Season chicken breasts with garlic powder, salt, and pepper. In a large skillet over medium heat, heat oil. Cook chicken until golden and cooked through, 8 minutes per side. Let rest 10 minutes, then cut into 1-inch pieces

3. Meanwhile, make dressing: In a medium bowl, whisk together oil, vinegar, Italian seasoning, garlic, and mustard. Season with salt and pepper.

4. In the large bowl with the pasta, toss together all remaining ingredients. Pour dressing over salad, toss until coated, and serve.

HOMEMADE FALAFEL

SERVES 10-12 • TOTAL TIME: 30 MIN

Falafel—fried chickpea balls—sound like something better left for your Middle Eastern takeout spot, but they're actually so easy to pull off. Delicious however you serve them: in a pita or tortilla, as a finger food with hummus, or over greens.

FOR THE FALAFELS

- 1 (15-ounce) can chickpeas, drained
- 4 cloves garlic, roughly chopped
- 1 shallot, roughly chopped
- 2 tablespoons freshly chopped parsley
- 1 teaspoon ground cumin
- 1 teaspoon ground coriander
- 3 tablespoons all-purpose flour
- Kosher salt
- Freshly ground black pepper
- Vegetable oil, for frying

FOR YOGURT SAUCE

- ½ cup Greek yogurt
- Juice of 1 lemon
- 1 tablespoon extra-virgin olive oil
- 1 tablespoon freshly chopped dill

FOR TAHINI SAUCE

- ½ cup tahini
- 1 clove garlic, minced
- 1 tablespoon lemon juice
- 2 tablespoons warm water

FOR SERVING

- Pitas
- Chopped lettuce
- Halved cherry tomatoes
- Thinly sliced cucumbers

1. In a food processor, combine chickpeas, garlic, shallot, parsley, cumin, coriander, and flour and season with salt and pepper. Pulse until mixture is coarse and mealy—do not over blend!

2. Form mixture into falafel balls about 2 inches in diameter, squeezing to compact. Transfer to chill in the refrigerator while oil heats.

3. In a pot, heat 1 inch of vegetable oil until a drop of water added to the oil sizzles and pops. Fry falafels until golden, then transfer to a paper towel–lined plate and season immediately with salt.

4. To make yogurt sauce: In a medium bowl, whisk together yogurt, lemon juice, oil, and dill. Season with salt and pepper.

5. To make tahini sauce: In a medium bowl, whisk together tahini, garlic, lemon juice, and warm water. Season with salt.

6. Serve falafels in pita with lettuce, tomatoes, and cucumber and drizzle with either sauce.

BUFFALO CHICKEN SALAD

SERVES 4 • TOTAL TIME: 1 HR

All of the bliss of eating wings, none of the saucy mess on your fingers. You'll want to keep a jar of this homemade ranch in your fridge at all times.

FOR THE CHICKEN

1 cup buffalo sauce

2 tablespoons honey

Juice of 1 lime

1 teaspoon garlic powder

½ teaspoon onion powder

Kosher salt

Freshly ground black pepper

1½ pounds boneless, skinless chicken breasts (about 3 breasts)

1 tablespoon extra-virgin olive oil

FOR THE DRESSING

½ cup mayonnaise

½ cup sour cream

½ cup buttermilk

2 cloves garlic, minced

¼ cup freshly chopped parsley

2 tablespoons freshly chopped dill

2 tablespoons freshly chopped chives

1½ teaspoons kosher salt

½ teaspoon freshly ground black pepper

½ teaspoon onion powder

Pinch of cayenne pepper

FOR THE SALAD

4 cups chopped romaine

2 cups baby spinach

2 stalks celery, sliced

1 carrot, cut into matchsticks

1 Persian cucumber, cut into half moons

1 avocado, sliced

½ red onion, thinly sliced

1 cup halved cherry tomatoes

¾ cup blue cheese crumbles

1. Make chicken: In a large bowl, combine buffalo sauce, honey, lime juice, garlic powder, and onion powder. Season with salt and pepper. Reserve ⅓ cup marinade. Add chicken to remaining marinade and toss to coat. Refrigerate for at least 30 minutes and up to 2 hours.

2. In a large skillet over medium heat, heat oil. Remove chicken from marinade, letting as much marinade drip off as possible, and add to skillet. Cook until golden, 6 minutes, then flip and brush chicken with reserved marinade. Continue cooking until no longer pink, 6 to 8 minutes more. Place on a cutting board and let rest 5 minutes, then slice into strips.

3. Meanwhile, make dressing: In a medium bowl, whisk together mayonnaise, sour cream, and buttermilk. Add remaining ingredients and stir until combined.

4. Assemble salad: In a large bowl, toss together all ingredients and drizzle with dressing.

BRUSCHETTA PASTA SALAD

SERVES 4 • TOTAL TIME: 25 MIN

Who says crostini gets to have all the fun with bruschetta? This salad is flawless for its simplicity. Gathering your favorite short-cut pasta (rigatoni, fusilli, even macaroni), the best cherry tomatoes you can find, and some fresh basil is pretty much half the work.

1 pound orecchiette

¼ cup extra-virgin olive oil

1 tablespoon balsamic vinegar

Kosher salt

Freshly ground black pepper

1 clove garlic, minced

1 pint cherry tomatoes, preferably multi-colored, halved

¼ cup torn basil, for garnish

1. In a large pot of salted boiling water, cook orecchiette according to package directions until al dente. Drain and set aside.

2. In a small bowl, whisk together olive oil and balsamic vinegar, then season with salt and pepper.

3. To bowl, add pasta, garlic and tomatoes; toss with dressing to combine.

4. Garnish with basil and serve.

HONEY-GARLIC CAULIFLOWER

SERVES 6 • TOTAL TIME: 35 MIN

We bake up a batch of this in the Delish kitchen on repeat—and no one has ever been able to resist a bite. The sweet and salty sauce of honey, soy sauce, garlic, and lime juice is a killer coating for the oven-crisped florets.

---

1 cup all-purpose flour

1 head cauliflower, chopped into bite-size florets

2 cups panko bread crumbs

3 large eggs, beaten

Kosher salt

Freshly ground black pepper

2 teaspoons cornstarch

⅓ cup honey

⅓ cup soy sauce

2 cloves garlic, minced

Juice of 1 lime

1 tablespoon Sriracha

¼ cup sliced scallions, for garnish

1. Preheat oven to 400° and line a large baking sheet with foil.

2. In a large bowl, combine flour and cauliflower, toss until fully coated. Set up a dredging station: In one bowl, add panko bread crumbs and in another bowl whisk eggs and add 2 tablespoons water. Dip cauliflower in beaten eggs, then panko until fully coated. Transfer to a prepared baking sheet and season generously with salt and pepper. Bake until golden and crispy, 20 to 25 minutes.

3. Meanwhile, make sauce: In a small bowl, whisk together cornstarch and ¼ cup water, until the cornstarch dissolves completely. Set aside. Combine honey, soy sauce, garlic, lime juice, and Sriracha in a small saucepan over medium heat. When the mixture reaches a boil, reduce heat and add the cornstarch mixture. Bring to simmer again and cook until sauce thickens, about 2 minutes.

4. Toss cooked cauliflower in sauce until evenly coated. Return the cauliflower to baking sheet and broil for 2 minutes.

5. Garnish with scallions and serve immediately.

BEST-EVER TUNA MELT

SERVES 3 • TOTAL TIME: 30 MIN

This has been known to convert even the strongest tuna hater. With the right amount of crunch—thanks to chopped celery, pickles, and red onion—and melty cheddar, this sandwich will become a regular in your rotation.

⅓ cup mayonnaise

Juice of ½ lemon

½ teaspoon crushed red pepper flakes (optional)

2 (6-ounce) cans tuna

1 rib celery, finely chopped

2 dill pickles, finely chopped

¼ cup finely chopped red onion

2 tablespoons freshly chopped parsley

Kosher salt

Freshly ground black pepper

8 slices bread, such as sourdough

2 tablespoons butter

1 tomato, sliced

8 slices cheddar

1. Preheat oven to 400°. In a large bowl, whisk together mayonnaise, lemon juice, and red pepper flakes (if using).

2. Drain tuna then add to mayonnaise mixture. Use a fork to break up tuna into flakes. Add celery, pickles, red onion, and parsley and toss to combine. Season with salt and pepper.

3. Butter one side of each bread slice. Top an unbuttered side with approximately ½ cup of tuna salad, 2 to 3 slices tomato, and 2 slices of cheese. Top with another slice of bread, buttered side facing up. Repeat with remaining ingredients and place on a large baking sheet. Bake until cheese is melty, 5 to 8 minutes.

CHAPTER THREE

DINNER

VEGETABLE SPAGHETTI

SERVES 6 • TOTAL TIME: 30 MIN

This is the perfect way to use up leftover veggies. Use whatever you have on hand—don't feel married to these specific ones. They are just a good starting point.

---

1 pound spaghetti

1 tablespoon extra-virgin olive oil

2 garlic cloves, minced

2 zucchini, sliced

1 carrot, chopped

1 red onion, thinly sliced

1 tablespoon tomato paste

1 (28-ounce) can diced tomatoes

1 teaspoon Italian seasoning

¼ teaspoon red pepper flakes

Kosher salt

Freshly ground black pepper

Sliced basil, for garnish

Freshly grated Parmesan, for garnish

1. In a large pot of boiling water, cook spaghetti according to package directions. Reserve 1 cup pasta water then drain spaghetti.

2. In a large skillet over medium heat, heat oil then add garlic and cook until fragrant, 1 minute. Add zucchini, carrot, and red onion and cook until soft, 7 minutes. Stir in tomato paste then add diced tomatoes and season with Italian seasoning, red pepper flakes, salt, and pepper, simmer 10 minutes.

3. Add spaghetti to skillet and ½ cup of reserved pasta water and toss to combine. Add more pasta water as necessary to bring sauce together.

4. Garnish with basil and Parmesan to serve.

LEMON RICOTTA PASTA

SERVES 4 • TOTAL TIME: 25 MIN

Once you're ready to graduate from spaghetti with butter and Parmesan, enroll in spaghetti with ricotta, olive oil, and lemon. Brighten it all up with a fresh herb; basil is a must during the summer, but parsley or chives do the trick, too.

---

1 pound bucatini or spaghetti

1 cup ricotta

½ cup extra-virgin olive oil

½ cup freshly grated pecorino or Parmesan

Zest and juice from 1 lemon

Kosher salt

Freshly ground black pepper

Red pepper flakes

Freshly sliced basil, for serving

1. In a large pot of boiling salted water, cook pasta according to package directions. Reserve 1 cup pasta water, then drain. Return pasta to pot.

2. In a medium bowl, combine ricotta, oil, pecorino, lemon juice, and zest. Season with salt, pepper, and a pinch of red pepper flakes. Add ricotta mixture and ¼ cup reserved pasta water to pasta and toss. Add more reserved pasta water if sauce is too thick.

3. Serve with basil, more pecorino, and a drizzle of olive oil.

PIZZA BURGERS

SERVES 4 • TOTAL TIME: 30 MIN

We're calling genius on this one. We simmer ground beef patties (try chicken or turkey, too) in marinara, then top them with mozz and pepperoni. Extra credit for brushing the buns with melted butter and topping with garlic and Parm for "garlic bread."

---

1 pound ground beef

2 cloves garlic, minced

¼ cup freshly chopped parsley

Kosher salt

Freshly ground black pepper

2 tablespoons vegetable oil

2½ cups marinara, divided

4 slices mozzarella

12 slices pepperoni

2 tablespoons melted butter

4 Kaiser rolls (or hamburger buns)

2 teaspoons garlic powder

1 teaspoon Italian seasoning

¼ cup freshly grated Parmesan

1. Preheat oven to 350°. In a medium bowl, combine ground beef, garlic, and parsley and mix with spatula until just combined. Using your hands, form 4 equally sized patties; season both sides with salt and pepper.

2. Heat oil in a large skillet over medium-high heat. Add burgers and cook, 4 to 5 minutes for medium. Flip patties, then immediately pour 2 cups marinara around them in pan. Reduce heat to medium-low and simmer for another minute, then top each with cheese and pepperoni slices. Cover pan and cook until cheese is melty and burger is cooked to your liking, about 3 minutes more.

3. Meanwhile, make garlic buns: Brush melted butter on inside of each half of the rolls and sprinkle with garlic powder, Italian seasoning, and Parmesan. Bake until golden, about 10 minutes.

4. Spread remaining ½ cup marinara on bottom buns followed by cooked burgers and the top bun halves.

CROCK-POT MAC & CHEESE

SERVES 8–10 · TOTAL TIME: 3 HR

Don't get us wrong: We live for a classic baked mac. But making a batch is a process (looking at you, roux). For the nights when you can but just don't want to, dump everything in the slow cooker, set it for two hours, and remind yourself how brilliant you are.

---

1 pound elbow macaroni

½ cup (1 stick) melted butter

4 cups shredded cheddar cheese

4 ounces cream cheese, cut into cubes

½ cup freshly grated Parmesan

2 (12-ounce) cans evaporated milk

2 cups whole milk

½ teaspoon garlic powder

⅛ teaspoon paprika

Kosher salt

Freshly ground black pepper

Finely chopped chives, for garnish (optional)

1. Combine macaroni, butter, cheddar cheese, cream cheese, Parmesan, evaporated milk, whole milk, garlic powder, and paprika in a slow cooker. Season with salt and pepper.

2. Cook on high until the pasta is cooked through and the sauce has thickened, 2 to 3 hours, checking after 2 hours, then every 20 minutes after.

3. Garnish with chives before serving, if using.

BEST-EVER BLACK BEAN BURGERS

SERVES 4 • TOTAL TIME: 1 HR 5 MIN

Let us take a guess: You've tasted more mushy and bland black bean burgers than enjoyable ones. Same—so we set out to create one you'll actually look forward to eating. Roasting the black beans dries them out and makes sure you end up with a sturdy patty, which we pack with mushrooms for umami.

---

2 (15-ounce) cans black beans, drained and rinsed

1 (3.5-ounce) package shiitake mushrooms, roughly chopped

½ yellow onion, thinly sliced

1 tablespoon extra-virgin olive oil

Kosher salt

Freshly ground black pepper

½ cup old-fashioned oats

½ avocado, chopped

¼ cup loosely packed cilantro or parsley leaves

2 cloves garlic, chopped

2 teaspoons smoked paprika

1 teaspoon chili powder

1 teaspoon ground cumin

Vegetable oil, for cooking

TOPPINGS

Toasted hamburger buns

Lettuce

Sliced red onion

Sliced avocado

Vegan or regular mayonnaise

1. Preheat oven to 375°. Spread beans in an even layer on a large baking sheet. Place mushrooms and onion on another large baking sheet and drizzle with olive oil. Season with salt and pepper and toss to coat, then spread in an even layer. Bake beans until they are dry and the skins are beginning to split, 7 to 9 minutes. Bake mushrooms and onions until tender, 18 to 20 minutes.

2. Add beans, mushrooms, and onion to the bowl of a food processor, along with oats, avocado, cilantro, garlic, paprika, chili powder, and cumin. Blend until smooth, scraping down sides of food processor as needed. Let mixture rest 10 minutes in refrigerator, then form into 4 patties.

3. In a large skillet over medium heat, heat enough vegetable oil to coat the bottom of the pan. Add veggie burgers to skillet and cook until outside is crisp and golden, and inside is heated through, about 4 minutes per side.

4. Assemble burgers with preferred toppings.

SHRIMP FETTUCCINE ALFREDO

SERVES 4 • TOTAL TIME: 25 MIN

For the nights when you want to feel like a boss. This pasta will make you feel like you're eating out at a fancy Italian restaurant, despite it taking less than a half hour to get on the table—that includes making from-scratch alfredo sauce; you'll never reach for the jarred stuff again.

---

1 pound fettuccine

3 tablespoons butter, divided

1 pound shrimp, peeled and deveined, tails removed

Kosher salt

Freshly ground black pepper

2 cloves garlic, minced

2 tablespoons all-purpose flour

1 cup heavy cream

½ cup whole milk

1 egg yolk

1 cup freshly grated Parmesan, plus more for garnish

1 tablespoon chopped parsley, for garnish

1. Cook fettuccine according to instructions on box, reserving a cup of pasta water to thicken the sauce, if needed.

2. In a large skillet over medium heat, heat 1 tablespoon butter until melted. Add shrimp, season with salt and pepper and cook until pink and completely opaque, 2 to 3 minutes per side. Remove shrimp from skillet and set aside.

3. Into the pan, add remaining 2 tablespoons butter and garlic. Cook until the garlic becomes fragrant, about 1 minute. Whisk in flour and cook until no longer raw, 2 minutes. Stir in heavy cream and milk, then whisk in egg yolk. Bring to a low simmer and whisk in Parmesan. When cheese is melted and sauce has thickened slightly, add cooked pasta and shrimp, tossing to combine. Season with salt and pepper.

4. Garnish with more Parmesan and parsley.

SPAGHETTI & MEATBALLS

SERVES 4 • TOTAL TIME: 1 HR

Dear Spaghetti and Meatballs,

Never change.

Our take on the Sunday-night classic doesn't skimp on the garlic, simmers in a three-ingredient sauce (onion! crushed tomatoes! bay leaf!), and absolutely requires sprinkling with lots of fresh Parm before digging in.

---

1 pound spaghetti

1 pound ground beef

⅓ cup bread crumbs

¼ cup finely chopped parsley

¼ cup freshly grated Parmesan, plus more for serving

1 egg

2 cloves garlic, minced

Kosher salt

½ teaspoon red pepper flakes

2 tablespoons extra-virgin olive oil

½ cup onion, finely chopped

1 (28-ounce) can crushed tomatoes

1 bay leaf

Freshly ground black pepper

1. In a large pot of boiling salted water, cook spaghetti according to package instructions. Drain.

2. In a large bowl, combine beef with bread crumbs, parsley, Parmesan, egg, garlic, 1 teaspoon salt, and red pepper flakes. Mix until just combined then form into 16 balls.

3. In a large pot over medium heat, heat oil. Add meatballs and cook, turning occasionally, until browned on all sides, about 10 minutes. Transfer meatballs to a plate.

4. Add onion to pot and cook until soft, 5 minutes. Add crushed tomatoes and bay leaf. Season with salt and pepper and bring to a simmer. Return meatballs to pot and cover. Simmer until sauce has thickened, 8 to 10 minutes.

5. Serve pasta with a healthy scoop of meatballs and sauce. Top with Parmesan before serving.

HONEY MUSTARD ROASTED SALMON

SERVES 6 · TOTAL TIME: 30 MIN

A dinner that checks all the boxes: Healthy ✔ Quick ✔ One dish ✔. Roasting a whole filet of salmon over a bed of citrus is one of our favorite prep methods. Slather on an addictive sauce of mustard, honey, and garlic and we guarantee it'll be one of yours, too.

Cooking spray
1 lemon sliced
1 (3–pound) salmon fillet
Kosher salt
Freshly ground black pepper
½ cup whole grain mustard
¼ cup extra–virgin olive oil

¼ cup honey
2 cloves garlic, minced
½ teaspoon red pepper flakes
Freshly chopped parsley,
   for serving

1. Preheat oven to 400° and grease a 9x13–inch baking dish with cooking spray. Place lemon slices on bottom of dish and place salmon on top. Season with salt and pepper.

2. In a medium bowl whisk together mustard, oil, honey, garlic, and red pepper flakes. Season with salt and pepper then pour sauce over salmon.

3. Roast salmon until cooked through and flakes easily with a fork, 20 minutes.

4. Turn oven to broil and broil another 5 minutes, if desired.

5. Garnish with parsley before serving.

ZUCCHINI LASAGNA ROLL-UPS

SERVES 4 · TOTAL TIME: 45 MIN

Q: Is there anything zucchini can't do?!

A: Nope. We've sliced the world's most versatile veg into lasagna noodles, and then rolled them up with marinara, ricotta, and mozzarella for a cheesy, saucy take on pasta.

---

6 large zucchini

1 (16-ounce) container ricotta

¾ cups freshly grated Parmesan, divided

2 large eggs

½ teaspoon garlic powder

Kosher salt

Freshly ground black pepper

1 cup marinara

1 cup grated mozzarella

1. Preheat oven to 400°. Slice zucchini lengthwise into ⅛-inch-thick strips, then place strips on a paper towel-lined baking sheet to drain.

2. Make ricotta mixture: In a small bowl, combine ricotta, ½ cup Parmesan, eggs, and garlic powder, and season with salt and pepper.

3. Spread a thin layer of marinara onto the bottom of a 9x13-inch baking dish. On each slice of zucchini, spoon a thin layer of sauce, spread ricotta mixture on top, and sprinkle with mozzarella. Roll up and place in baking dish, packed together tightly.

4. Sprinkle with remaining ¼ cup Parmesan. Bake until zucchini is tender and cheese is melty, 20 minutes.

CHICKEN PRIMAVERA SPAGHETTI SQUASH BOATS

SERVES 2 • TOTAL TIME: 1 HR

Who can say no to veggies when they're this fun to eat? First they're sautéed with garlic and lemon, then spooned into roasted halves of spaghetti squash, and then topped with two different kinds of cheese for a fully loaded healthy dinner.

FOR SPAGHETTI SQUASH

1 medium spaghetti squash,
  halved, seeds removed

1 tablespoon extra-virgin olive oil

Kosher salt

Freshly ground black pepper

**FOR PRIMAVERA FILLING +
TOPPING**

1 tablespoon extra-virgin olive oil

½ small red onion, chopped

1 orange bell pepper, chopped

1 cup grape tomatoes, halved

1 medium zucchini, cut into
  half moons

2 cloves garlic, minced

1 teaspoon lemon zest

½ teaspoon Italian seasoning

2½ cups cooked shredded chicken

1 cup shredded mozzarella

¼ cup freshly grated Parmesan

Freshly chopped parsley,
  for garnish

1. Preheat oven to 400°. Drizzle cut sides of spaghetti squash with oil and season with salt and pepper. Place cut side down on a large, rimmed baking sheet. Roast until tender, 30 to 35 minutes. Let cool slightly. Using a fork, break up squash strands.

2. Meanwhile, make primavera filling: In a large skillet over medium heat, heat oil. Add onion and pepper and cook until mostly tender, 3 to 4 minutes, then add tomatoes, zucchini, garlic, and lemon zest. Season with salt, pepper, and Italian seasoning and cook 3 to 4 minutes more. Stir in chicken and remove from heat.

3. Divide mixture between spaghetti squash halves and stir to combine. Top each spaghetti squash with cheese and return to oven to melt, 5 minutes.

4. Top with Parmesan and parsley to serve.

PRIMAVERA SKILLET PIZZA

SERVES 2 • TOTAL TIME: 45 MIN

Yet another reason we love our cast–iron: Baking pizza dough in it produces the crispiest, oil–slicked crust. While the dough comes to room temperature, roast a sheet tray of whatever veggies you have in the fridge. We skip a sauce altogether and instead go for ricotta and olive oil, which will please any pizza lover.

---

2 bell peppers, sliced

½ head broccoli, florets removed

¼ small red onion, thinly sliced

1 cup cherry tomatoes

Extra-virgin olive oil

Kosher salt

Freshly ground black pepper

All-purpose flour, for dusting surface

½ pound pizza dough, at room temperature

1 cup ricotta

1 cup shredded mozzarella

1. Heat oven to 400°. On a large baking sheet, toss peppers, broccoli, onion, and cherry tomatoes with olive oil and season with salt and pepper.

2. Roast until tender and tomatoes are bursting, 18 to 20 minutes. Remove and increase oven temperature to 500°.

3. Meanwhile, brush an oven-proof skillet with olive oil.

4. On a floured work surface, use your hands to roll out dough until it's the circumference of your skillet. Transfer to skillet and brush dough all over with olive oil.

5. Leaving a ½-inch border for crust, dollop spoonfuls of ricotta on dough and sprinkle with mozzarella.

6. Top with roasted vegetables and drizzle with olive oil. Sprinkle crust with salt.

7. Bake until crust is crispy and cheese is melted, about 12 minutes.

SPICED CHICKEN TACOS

SERVES 4 • TOTAL TIME: 30 MIN

Proof Taco Tuesday should be every day. The chicken is unreal—thanks to the generous amount of chili and garlic powders, cumin, and paprika that blankets it. The easiest way to toast a tortilla? Place a tortilla directly over the flame until charred (keep an eye on it!) if you have a gas range; toast them in a skillet if you have electric.

---

3 tablespoons extra-virgin olive oil

4 boneless, skinless chicken breasts, cut into 1-inch strips

Kosher salt

Freshly ground black pepper

2 teaspoons chili powder

2 teaspoons cumin

½ teaspoon garlic powder

¼ teaspoon paprika

¼ teaspoon cayenne

8 corn tortillas, warmed

Lime wedges, for serving

TACO TOPPING OPTIONS

Thinly sliced red onion

Diced tomatoes

Shredded Monterey jack

Diced avocados

Fresh cilantro

---

1. In a large skillet over medium heat, heat oil. Season chicken with salt and pepper and add to skillet. Cook until golden, 6 minutes. Add spices and stir until coated, 1 minute more.

2. Build tacos: In tortillas, layer chicken and desired toppings. Serve with lime wedges.

PRO TIP!

Want to sub in brown rice? Up the chicken broth by ½ cup.

CHEESY CHICKEN BROCCOLI BAKE

SERVES 4 · TOTAL TIME: 50 MIN

Bookmark this one-dish wonder for any night you're too lazy for clean-up. You sear the chicken breasts and simmer the rice all in one skillet. The only time you turn on the oven is for a last-minute broil so the cheddar and bread crumbs take on some crunch.

- 1 tablespoon extra-virgin olive oil
- 1 cup small yellow onion, chopped
- 2 cloves garlic, minced
- 1 pound boneless, skinless chicken breasts, cut into 1-inch pieces
- Kosher salt
- Freshly ground black pepper
- 1 cup white rice
- 1 cup heavy cream
- 2½ cups low-sodium chicken broth, divided
- 2 cups broccoli florets
- 1 cup shredded cheddar
- ¼ cup panko bread crumbs

1. In a large oven-safe skillet over medium-high heat, heat oil. Add onion and cook, stirring, until soft, 5 minutes. Add garlic and cook until fragrant, 1 minute more. Add chicken and season with salt and pepper. Cook, stirring occasionally, until golden, about 6 minutes more.

2. Stir in rice, heavy cream, and 1 cup of the broth. Bring to a simmer and cook until rice is tender, about 15 minutes. Add remaining 1½ cups broth, broccoli, and cheddar cheese and cook until broccoli is tender and cheese is melty, about 10 minutes.

3. Heat broiler. Sprinkle chicken mixture with bread crumbs and season with salt and pepper. Broil until golden and crispy, about 2 minutes.

SALMON FISH STICKS WITH ZUCCHINI CHIPS

SERVES 4 · TOTAL TIME: 1 HR

Fish sticks the whole family can get behind. These are all about the bright, garlicky sun-dried tomato dipping sauce. To get the zucchini blissfully crispy, slice them as thinly as you possibly can.

Extra-virgin olive oil

1 cup sun-dried tomatoes, oil drained and chopped

1 clove garlic, minced

Kosher salt

Freshly ground black pepper

2 cups crushed tomatoes

2 tablespoons heavy cream

5 large zucchini, sliced into ⅛-inch rounds

1½ pounds skinless salmon, cut into 1-inch strips

Canola oil, for frying

2 cups panko bread crumbs

1 egg

1 cup all-purpose flour

Sea salt, such as Maldon

¼ cup chopped fresh parsley

1. Preheat oven to 425°. Line two sheet pans with parchment paper and insert wire racks. In a medium pot, heat 1 tablespoon olive oil over medium heat. Add sun-dried tomatoes and garlic; season with ½ teaspoon salt and ¼ teaspoon black pepper. Cook until garlic is softened, 2 minutes. Add crushed tomatoes and heavy cream and heat through, 5 minutes. Using an immersion blender, pulse until sauce is smooth. Turn off heat and cover sauce to keep warm.

2. Using a mandolin, slice zucchini into thin rounds approximately ⅛-inch thick. Spread zucchini into an even layer over the sheet pans. Drizzle with olive oil and season with salt and pepper. Roast until golden brown, 25 to 30 minutes.

3. Meanwhile, preheat cast iron skillet with 1 inch canola oil over medium-high heat. Prepare breading station with three medium bowls: one bowl with panko, another with egg and 1 tablespoon water, beaten, and the third with flour. Season fish with salt and pepper. Coat each piece of fish with flour and shake off excess, then dip in egg and coat in breadcrumbs. Fry fish in two batches until golden brown, about 2 minutes. Drain and transfer to a paper towel-lined plate. Season with salt immediately.

4. Serve fish sticks with zucchini chips and ramekin of sundried tomato sauce. Garnish with sea salt and parsley.

OVEN-BAKED BBQ RIBS

SERVES 4 · TOTAL TIME: 2 HR 20 MIN

The easiest way to make super-tender, flavorful ribs any time of the year (don't @ us). They're sticky, they're sweet, and everyone we know devours them.

FOR THE RIBS

- 2 pounds baby back ribs
- ½ cup packed brown sugar
- 2 teaspoons kosher salt
- 1 tablespoon garlic powder
- ½ teaspoon freshly ground black pepper
- ½ teaspoon paprika
- ½ teaspoon ground mustard
- ¼ teaspoon cayenne

FOR THE BARBECUE SAUCE

- 1½ cups ketchup
- 1 cup packed brown sugar
- ½ cup water
- ¼ cup apple cider vinegar
- 1 tablespoon Worcestershire sauce
- 1 tablespoon molasses
- 1 teaspoon kosher salt
- ½ teaspoon garlic powder
- ½ teaspoon onion powder
- ¼ teaspoon ground mustard
- ¼ teaspoon paprika

1. Preheat oven to 300° and line a baking sheet with aluminum foil. Remove thin membrane on the backside by sliding a knife under the membrane, then peel it away.

2. In a small bowl, stir together sugar, salt, and spices. Rub mixture all over ribs and place on prepared baking sheet. Cover with foil and bake until very tender, 2 hours.

3. Meanwhile make barbecue sauce: In a medium saucepan over medium heat, combine all sauce ingredients together. Bring to a boil, then reduce heat and let simmer, stirring occasionally, until thickened, 1 hour.

4. Turn oven to broil. Remove foil from ribs and brush both sides with barbecue sauce. Broil until sauce just starts to caramelize, 2 to 4 minutes.

CHICKEN FAJITAS

SERVES 6 • TOTAL TIME: 50 MIN

A Tex-Mex dinner so easy even the kids can make it. Marinating the chicken even for just a half hour in olive oil, lime juice, cumin, and red pepper flakes makes it feel special, but if you're in a hurry, keep it moving.

½ cup plus 1 tablespoon extra-virgin olive oil

¼ cup lime juice, from about 3 limes

2 teaspoons cumin

½ teaspoon crushed red pepper flakes

1 pound boneless, skinless chicken breasts

Kosher salt

Freshly ground black pepper

2 bell peppers, thinly sliced

1 large onion, thinly sliced

Tortillas, for serving

---

1. In a large bowl, whisk together ½ cup oil, lime juice, cumin, and red pepper flakes. Season chicken with salt and pepper, then add to bowl and toss to coat. Let marinate in the fridge at least 30 minutes and up to 2 hours.

2. When ready to cook, heat remaining tablespoon oil in a large skillet over medium heat. Add chicken and cook until golden and cooked through, 8 minutes per side. Let rest 10 minutes, then slice into strips.

3. Add bell peppers and onion to skillet and cook until soft, 5 minutes. Add chicken and toss until combined. Serve with tortillas.

GRILLED PINEAPPLE CHICKEN

SERVES 4 · TOTAL TIME: 2 HR 25 MIN

Transport yourself somewhere tropical with this sweet barbecued chicken. Pineapple juice helps tenderize the meat and the brown sugar gets nice and caramelized on the grill. Haven't thrown pineapple on the grill before? Now's the time.

- **1 cup unsweetened pineapple juice**
- **¾ cup ketchup**
- **½ cup low-sodium soy sauce**
- **½ cup brown sugar**
- **2 cloves garlic, minced**
- **1 tablespoon freshly minced ginger**
- **1 pound boneless, skinless chicken breasts**
- **1 teaspoon vegetable oil, plus more for grill**
- **1 pineapple, sliced into rings and halved**
- **Thinly sliced green onions, for garnish**

1. In a large bowl, whisk together pineapple juice, ketchup, soy sauce, brown sugar, garlic, and ginger until combined.

2. Add chicken to a large resealable plastic bag and pour in marinade. Let marinate in the fridge at least 2 hours and up to overnight.

3. When ready to grill, heat grill to high. Oil grates and grill chicken, basting with marinade, until charred and cooked through, 8 minutes per side.

4. Toss pineapple with oil and grill until charred, 2 minutes per side.

5. Garnish chicken and pineapple with green onions before serving.

BROCCOLI CHEDDAR SOUP

SERVES 4 • TOTAL TIME: 50 MIN

Panera fans, we got you. This copycat recipe is the ultimate way to warm up on a cold night. Change up the cheese based on whatever your family loves; a blend of cheddar, fontina, and Swiss is great here, too.

---

4 tablespoons butter

1 onion, chopped

¼ cup all-purpose flour

2 cups low-sodium chicken broth

Kosher salt

Freshly ground black pepper

1 large head broccoli, finely chopped

1 large carrot, grated

2 stalks celery, thinly sliced

2 cups whole milk

3 cups shredded cheddar, plus more for garnish

Baguette, for serving

1. In a large pot over medium heat, melt butter. Add onion and cook until soft, 5 minutes. Whisk in flour and let cook 2 minutes. Add chicken broth and season generously with salt and pepper.

2. Stir in broccoli, carrots, and celery. Bring to a boil and reduce heat to low. Let simmer until vegetables are tender, 20 minutes.

3. Add milk and bring to a simmer, then stir in cheddar.

4. Season with salt and pepper and top with more cheddar. Serve with baguette.

HAMBURGER SOUP

SERVES 6 · TOTAL TIME: 45 MIN

In this play off a burger, ground beef simmers in a tomato-y broth, potatoes sub in for fries, and yellow mustard adds a little zing (and that signature flavor). For the full effect, topping with bread and butter pickles is not optional.

---

1 tablespoon extra-virgin olive oil

1 pound ground beef

Kosher salt

Freshly ground black pepper

1 small yellow onion, chopped

2 medium Yukon gold potatoes, peeled and cut into ½-inch cubes

2 medium carrots, thinly sliced into coins

2 stalks celery, thinly sliced

4 cloves garlic, minced

2 tablespoons tomato paste

4 cups low-sodium beef or chicken broth

1 (14.5-ounce) can diced tomatoes

1 teaspoon Italian seasoning

½ cup frozen corn

1 teaspoon yellow mustard

Freshly chopped parsley, for garnish

Bread and butter pickles, for serving

1. In a large pot over medium-high heat, heat oil. Add ground beef and cook, breaking up with a spoon, until golden, about 8 minutes. Season with salt and pepper. Using a slotted spoon, remove the beef to a plate.

2. To the same pot, add the onion, potatoes, carrots, celery, and garlic and season with salt and pepper. Cook, stirring occasionally, until vegetables are soft, about 5 minutes. Add the tomato paste and cook, stirring, 1 minute.

3. Return the beef to the pot. Pour in broth and diced tomatoes, with juices, stir to combine. Add the Italian seasoning and bring to a boil. Cook until potatoes are tender, about 10 minutes.

4. Stir in corn and mustard and cook until warm, 1 minute more. Season with salt and pepper to taste.

5. Garnish with parsley and pickles before serving.

DECONSTRUCTED LASAGNA

SERVES 4 • TOTAL TIME: 25 MIN

Everyone will be fighting over who gets to smash the lasagna noodles with the rolling pin (seriously, it's a stress reliever). No sauce required: Simply top the cooked pasta with peas, dollops of ricotta, fresh mint, and a drizzle of olive oil and you're done.

---

1 pound lasagna noodles

Kosher salt

2 tablespoons extra-virgin olive oil, plus more for drizzling

1 cup small onion, chopped

2 cloves garlic, minced

1 cup low-sodium chicken broth

1 pound peas (fresh or frozen)

½ cup chopped parsley

1½ cups freshly grated pecorino Romano, divided

1½ cups whole milk ricotta

½ cup mint leaves

Freshly ground black pepper

1. Bring a large pot of water to a boil and generously season with salt. Place lasagna noodles in resealable plastic bag on top of a kitchen towel and gently break up noodles using a rolling pin. (Shapes can be all different sizes.) Cook pasta according to package instructions until al dente. Drain, reserving 1 cup pasta water, and return to pot.

2. Meanwhile, in a large skillet over medium heat, heat oil. Add onion and garlic and cook until onion is softened, about 5 minutes. Pour in chicken broth and season with salt, then bring to a boil and simmer for 5 minutes. Add peas and stir until warmed through.

3. Add cooked lasagna noodles, parsley and 1 cup pecorino to skillet and mix until pasta is well coated. (If pasta is dry, add a splash of reserved pasta water.)

4. Transfer pasta mixture to a large platter. Add large spoonfuls of ricotta all over and top with fresh mint, pepper, remaining ½ cup pecorino, and a drizzle of olive oil. Serve immediately.

BEEF & BROCCOLI

SERVES 4 · TOTAL TIME: 40 MIN

This spin on a Chinese–American classic calls for brown sugar (for a little bit of sweetness), lime juice (for a fresh tang), and Sriracha (for a touch of spiciness). If you want to give it a more trademark take–out flavor, you'll want to stir in a couple tablespoons of hoisin, a fermented bean paste, when you add the soy sauce.

⅔ cup low-sodium
   soy sauce, divided

Juice of ½ lime

3 tablespoons packed
   brown sugar, divided

2 tablespoons cornstarch,
   divided

Kosher salt

Freshly ground black pepper

1 pound sirloin steak, sliced
   thinly against grain

2 tablespoons vegetable oil

3 cloves garlic, minced

⅓ cup low-sodium
   beef broth

2 teaspoons Sriracha
   (optional)

1 head broccoli, cut
   into florets

Sesame seeds, for garnish

Thinly sliced green onions,
   for garnish

1. In a medium bowl, whisk ⅓ cup soy sauce, lime juice, 1 tablespoon brown sugar, and 1 tablespoon cornstarch until combined. Add steak, season with salt and pepper, and toss until steak is coated. Marinate 20 minutes.

2. In a large skillet over medium–high heat, heat oil. Add steak in a single layer, working in batches if needed, and cook until seared, about 2 minutes per side. Remove steak and set aside.

3. Stir in garlic and cook until fragrant, about 1 minute. Stir in remaining 1 tablespoon cornstarch until garlic is coated, then stir in broth, remaining 2 tablespoons brown sugar, remaining ⅓ cup soy sauce, and Sriracha (if using). Bring mixture to a simmer. Add broccoli and simmer until tender, about 5 minutes. Season sauce with salt and pepper (if necessary), then return steak to skillet.

4. Garnish with sesame seeds and green onions before serving.

COCONUT CURRY CHICKEN

SERVES 5 • TOTAL TIME: 35 MIN

Coconut curry chicken has TONS of variations; from South India to Thailand, no two curries are exactly the same. Our Americanized version might be a bit untraditional, but trust us, it's delicious.

---

1 tablespoon vegetable oil

1 tablespoon butter

1 medium red onion, chopped

2 large shallots, minced

Kosher salt

2 cloves garlic, minced

1 teaspoon freshly grated ginger

1½ tablespoons curry powder

2 tablespoons tomato paste

1 (13-ounce) can coconut milk

½ cup water

1½ pounds boneless, skinless chicken breast, cut into 1-inch pieces

Juice of ½ lime

Lime wedges, for serving

Mint leaves, torn, for serving

Cilantro leaves, torn, for serving

Cooked rice, for serving

1. In a large pot or high-sided skillet over medium heat, heat oil and butter. When butter is melted, add onion and shallots and cook until tender and translucent, 6 to 8 minutes.

2. Add garlic, ginger, and curry powder and cook until fragrant, 1 minute more. Add tomato paste and cook until darkened slightly, 1 to 2 minutes more.

3. Add coconut milk and water and bring to a simmer. Add chicken and cook, stirring occasionally, until chicken is cooked through, 6 to 8 minutes.

4. Stir in lime juice and garnish with mint and cilantro. Serve hot with rice.

CHAPTER 4

VEGGIES

AVOCADO & TOMATO SALAD

Guacamole masquerading as a salad—dreams do come true. Cumin, lemon juice, and a hefty glug of olive oil deliver tons of flavor. Oh, and yes, it's totally acceptable to dig in with tortilla chips.

¼ cup extra-virgin olive oil

Juice of 1 lemon

¼ teaspoon cumin

Kosher salt

Freshly ground black pepper

3 avocados, cubed

1 pint cherry tomatoes, halved

1 small cucumber, sliced into half moons

⅓ cup corn

1 jalepeño, minced (optional)

2 tablespoons chopped cilantro

1. In a small bowl, whisk together oil, lime juice, and cumin. Season dressing with salt and pepper.

2. In a large serving bowl, combine avocados, tomatoes, cucumber, corn, jalapeño (if using), and cilantro. Gently toss with dressing and serve immediately.

GARLIC-PARM ZUCCHINI SAUTÉ

SERVES 4 · TOTAL TIME: 20 MIN

Got extra zucchini? Then you gotta make this. The squash deepens in flavor as it crisps up and caramelizes in your cast iron skillet; all it needs is a hit of fresh Parm to rock your world.

1 tablespoon extra-virgin olive oil
2 cloves garlic, minced
3 large zucchini, cut into rounds
½ teaspoon dried oregano
Kosher salt

Freshly ground black pepper
Crushed red pepper flakes
¼ cup freshly grated Parmesan

1. In a large skillet over medium heat, heat oil. Add garlic and cook until fragrant, 30 seconds. Add zucchini and oregano. Cook until zucchini is tender, about 10 minutes. Season with salt, pepper, and a pinch red pepper flakes.

2. Top with Parmesan and serve warm.

HONEY-GLAZED CARROTS

SERVES 6 · TOTAL TIME: 45 MIN

Two words: honey butter. This stupid-simple recipe gives you stupid-delicious results. Tossing the carrots in a melted butter mixture of honey, rosemary, and garlic gets them nice and glaze-y in the oven—and brings out their natural sweetness. No one will see this veg the same way again.

¼ cup butter

2 tablespoons honey

½ teaspoon dried rosemary

½ teaspoon garlic powder

Kosher salt

Freshly ground black pepper

15 carrots (2 pounds), peeled and halved lengthwise

Fresh thyme, for garnish (optional)

1. Preheat oven to 400°. In a saucepan over low heat, melt butter. Stir in honey, rosemary, and garlic powder and season with salt and pepper.

2. Place carrots on a large baking sheet. Pour over glaze and toss until coated.

3. Roast until caramelized and glazed, 35 to 40 minutes.

4. Garnish with thyme, if desired, before serving.

CHEESY SCALLOPED ZUCCHINI

SERVES 6 • TOTAL TIME: 45 MIN

Sign us up for scalloped anything. This twist on a classic potato gratin still has all the indulgent butter, milk, Gruyère, and Parm, but none of the carbs. Gruyère can be complex and earthy; milder Havarti or fontina are solid subs.

2 tablespoons butter, plus more for buttering pan

2 cloves garlic, minced

2 tablespoons all-purpose flour

1½ cups whole milk

2 cups shredded Gruyère, divided

½ cup freshly grated Parmesan

Kosher salt

Freshly ground black pepper

Pinch nutmeg

4 medium zucchini, sliced crosswise into ¼-inch coins

2 teaspoons freshly chopped thyme

Freshly chopped parsley, for garnish

1. Preheat oven to 375° and butter a medium casserole dish. In a large skillet over medium heat, melt butter. Add garlic and cook until fragrant, about 1 minute. Whisk in flour and cook until flour is golden and starts to bubble, about 1 minute more. Add milk and stir until mixture comes to a simmer. Boil until slightly thickened, about 1 minute.

2. Turn off heat and add 1 cup Gruyère and Parmesan. Stir until cheese has melted, then season with salt, pepper, and nutmeg.

3. Add a layer of zucchini to the baking dish, overlapping the zucchini slices. Season with salt and pepper and pour about one-third of the cream mixture over zucchini. Sprinkle some of the remaining Gruyère on top, then sprinkle thyme on top of cheese.

4. Make two more layers with remaining zucchini slices, cream mixture, cheese and thyme. Bake until bubbly and golden on top, 23 to 25 minutes.

5. Garnish with parsley and serve warm.

CHEESY BACON BUTTERNUT SQUASH

SERVES 6 • TOTAL TIME: 45 MIN

The one thing that manages to make the sweet flavor of butternut squash even better? Bacon (duh). We even decided to top off everything with some melty mozzarella and salty Parm because we're extra like that.

---

2 pounds butternut squash, peeled and cut into 1-inch pieces

2 tablespoons olive oil

2 cloves garlic, minced

2 tablespoons chopped thyme

Kosher salt

Freshly ground black pepper

½ pound bacon, chopped

1½ cups shredded mozzarella

½ cup freshly grated Parmesan

Chopped fresh parsley, for garnish

1. Preheat oven to 425°. In a large ovenproof skillet (or in a large baking dish), toss butternut squash with olive oil, garlic and thyme. Season with salt and pepper, then scatter bacon on top.

2. Bake until the squash is tender and the bacon is cooked through, 20 to 25 minutes.

3. Remove skillet from oven and top with mozzarella and Parmesan. Bake for another 5 to 10 minutes, or until the cheese is melty.

4. Garnish with parsley and serve warm.

MEXICAN CORN SALAD

SERVES 4 · TOTAL TIME: 25 MIN

A riff on "elote"—cobs of corn dressed up with mayo, lime juice, and cotija sold on the streets in Mexico. Creamy, salty, and citrusy, this salad will be devoured at every potluck, cookout, or picnic. When fresh corn isn't in season, sub in frozen kernels.

6 ears corn

Kosher salt

½ cup mayonnaise

¼ cup cotija cheese or feta, plus more for garnish

Juice of 2 limes

2 tablespoons chopped fresh cilantro, plus more for garnish

1 tablespoon chili powder, plus more for garnish

1. Using a sharp knife, carefully cut corn kernels off cob. Add about ½ inch water to a medium saucepan and salt well. Bring to a simmer. Add corn, cover, and cook until corn is tender, 3 to 4 minutes. Drain and pat dry.

2. In a serving bowl, toss corn with mayonnaise, cotija, lime juice, cilantro, and chili powder. Season generously with salt.

3. Top with more cotija, cilantro, and a sprinkle of chili powder before serving.

CAULIFLOWER TOTS

SERVES 6 • TOTAL TIME: 30 MIN

TBH these cheesy nuggets might be better than the real thing. Steaming the cauli (and wringing out its moisture) is key here: The drier and more tender the riced cauliflower is, the better your tots will bake up.

Cooking spray

4 cups cauliflower florets, steamed (about ½ large cauliflower)

1 large egg, lightly beaten

1 cup shredded cheddar

1 cup freshly grated Parmesan

⅔ cup panko bread crumbs

2 tablespoons freshly chopped chives

Kosher salt

Freshly ground black pepper

½ cup ketchup

2 tablespoons Sriracha

1. Preheat oven to 375°. Grease a large baking sheet with cooking spray.

2. In a food processor, pulse steamed cauliflower until riced. Place riced cauliflower on a clean kitchen towel and squeeze to drain water.

3. Transfer cauliflower to a large bowl with egg, cheddar, Parmesan, panko, and chives and mix until combined. Season with salt and pepper to taste.

4. Spoon about 1 tablespoon mixture and roll it into a tater-tot shape with your hands. Place on prepared baking sheet and bake for 15 to 20 minutes, until tots are golden.

5. Meanwhile, make spicy ketchup: Combine ketchup and Sriracha in a small serving bowl and stir to combine.

6. Serve warm cauliflower tots with spicy ketchup.

AIR FRYER SWEET POTATO FRIES

SERVES 2 • TOTAL TIME: 50 MIN

The first time we air-fried, we were SHOCKED at how crispy stuff got. Oven-baked fries simply can't stack up. This three-ingredient fry sauce might be the real star here though; skip the hot sauce if you prefer less heat.

2 medium sweet potatoes, peeled and cut into ¼-inch sticks

1 tablespoon extra-virgin olive oil

½ teaspoon garlic powder

½ teaspoon chili powder

Kosher salt

Freshly ground black pepper

2 tablespoons mayonnaise

2 tablespoons barbecue sauce

1 teaspoon hot sauce, such as Texas Pete

1. In a large bowl, toss sweet potatoes with oil and spices. Season with salt and pepper.

2. Working in batches, spread an even layer of sweet potato fries in air fryer basket. Cook at 375° for 8 minutes, flip fries, then cook 8 minutes more.

3. Meanwhile, make dipping sauce: In a medium bowl, whisk to combine mayonnaise, barbecue sauce, and hot sauce.

4. Serve fries with sauce on the side for dipping.

BACON ZUCCHINI FRIES

SERVES 8 · TOTAL TIME: 50 MIN

We call 'em fries, you might call 'em bacon–wrapped zucchini wedges. Whatever the name, they'll be gone in minutes. As the squash roasts, it takes on an intense bacon flavor and turns to velvet.

Cooking spray
4 zucchini, cut into wedges
16 strips bacon
Ranch, for serving

1. Preheat oven to 425° and spray a baking sheet with cooking spray. Wrap each zucchini wedge in bacon and place on baking sheet.

2. Bake until the bacon is cooked through and crispy, about 35 minutes. Serve with ranch.

CREAMED BRUSSELS SPROUTS

SERVES 6 • TOTAL TIME: 1 HR 15 MIN

Creamed spinach can feel a little old school, but creamed Brussels sprouts?! Yes, please. This veggie bake gets its silky texture from Greek yogurt, mayo, and two types of cheese. Lemon zest makes the whole thing pop.

1 tablespoon extra-virgin olive oil

½ large yellow onion, chopped

3 cloves garlic, minced

2 pounds Brussels sprouts, halved and thinly sliced

½ teaspoon crushed red pepper flakes, plus more for garnish

Kosher salt

Freshly ground black pepper

1 cup Greek yogurt

½ cup mayonnaise

2 eggs, lightly beaten

Zest of ½ lemon

½ cup freshly shredded fontina

½ cup freshly grated Parmesan, plus more for garnish

2 tablespoons freshly chopped parsley

1. Heat oven to 375°. In a large skillet over medium heat, heat oil. Add onions and cook until soft, 6 minutes. Add garlic and cook until fragrant, 1 minute. Add Brussels sprouts and red pepper flakes and cook until tender, 7 minutes more. Season with salt and pepper, then remove from heat and let cool.

2. In a large bowl, stir together Greek yogurt, mayonnaise, eggs, lemon zest, and cheeses and season with salt and pepper. Fold in cooled vegetables and transfer to a medium baking dish.

3. Bake until top is golden and cheese is bubbly, 30 to 35 minutes.

4. Garnish with parsley, Parmesan, and red pepper flakes and serve immediately.

SMASHED BRUSSELS SPROUTS

SERVES 6–8 • TOTAL TIME: 55 MIN

Just when you think you've tried all the ways the beloved Brussels sprout can be prepped—roasted! shaved! fried!—we introduce the smash. Like with smashed potatoes, you need to boil these first before getting to the action. Once smashed, pat them as dry as you can, so they crisp nicely in the oven.

2 pounds Brussels sprouts

2 tablespoons extra-virgin olive oil

2 cloves garlic, minced

1 teaspoon freshly chopped thyme

Kosher salt

Freshly ground black pepper

1 cup shredded mozzarella

¼ cup freshly grated Parmesan

Freshly chopped parsley, for garnish

1. Preheat oven to 425° and line a large baking sheet with parchment paper. Prepare an ice bath in a large bowl.

2. Blanch Brussels sprouts: Bring a large pot of salted water to a boil. Add Brussels sprouts and cook until bright green and very tender, 8 to 10 minutes. Add Brussels sprouts to ice bath to cool then drain and pat dry.

3. On a large baking sheet, toss blanched Brussels sprouts with oil, garlic, and thyme. Using the end of a small glass or mason jar, press down on Brussels sprouts to smash them into a flat patty. Season each smashed Brussels sprout with salt and pepper, then sprinkle mozzarella and Parmesan on top.

4. Bake until bottoms of sprouts are crispy and cheese is melty and golden, 20 to 25 minutes.

5. Garnish with parsley and serve warm.

GRILLED BROCCOLI

SERVES 6 • TOTAL TIME: 25 MIN

Ketchup on broccoli? Oh yes. The sweet, savory flavor of every kid's favorite condiment pairs weirdly well with the other ingredients happening here: Worcestershire, soy sauce, and honey. Just trust us.

---

2 pounds broccoli

¼ cup extra-virgin olive oil

2 tablespoons Worcestershire sauce

1 tablespoon low-sodium soy sauce

3 tablespoons ketchup

1 tablespoon honey

3 cloves garlic, minced

½ teaspoon kosher salt, plus more for sprinkling

Freshly ground black pepper

¼ teaspoon crushed red pepper flakes, plus more for serving

¼ cup freshly grated Parmesan

Lemon wedges, for serving

---

1. Preheat grill to medium heat. Trim off fibrous bottom half of broccoli stem, then quarter broccoli head into small trees.

2. In a large bowl, whisk together oil, Worcestershire, soy sauce, ketchup, honey, and garlic. Season with salt, pepper, and red pepper flakes. Add in broccoli and toss to coat. Let sit for 10 minutes.

3. Place broccoli on grill and sprinkle lightly with more salt. Grill broccoli until knife-tender and slightly charred, flipping every 2 minutes and basting with any remaining sauce, 8 to 10 minutes.

4. Sprinkle with Parmesan and more red pepper flakes, and serve with lemon wedges.

MASHED BUTTERNUT SQUASH

Mashed squash > mashed potatoes. We can't get over how, well, naturally buttery the butternut gets from hanging out in the oven for a half hour. Blending it up with some butter makes it outta this world.

2 (2-pound) butternut squash, peeled, seeded, and cut into 1-inch cubes

4 tablespoons extra-virgin olive oil

Kosher salt

Freshly ground black pepper

4 tablespoons butter

Cayenne pepper, for garnish (optional)

1. Preheat oven to 400°. On a large baking sheet, toss butternut squash with oil and season with salt and pepper.

2. Roast until squash is extremely tender, tossing halfway through, about 30 minutes.

3. Place squash and butter into the bowl of a food processor and blend until smooth.

4. Serve with a pinch of cayenne pepper, if using.

LOADED CAULIFLOWER SALAD

SERVES 6 • TOTAL TIME: 30 MIN

Don't worry, everything you love about potato salad is still here: bacon, sour cream, cheddar, and chives. We steam the cauli to get the florets tender, but if you have extra time and want them to take on even more flavor, roasting is great, too.

1 large head cauliflower, cut into florets

6 slices bacon

½ cup sour cream

¼ cup mayonnaise

1 tablespoon lemon juice

½ teaspoon garlic powder

Kosher salt

Freshly ground black pepper

1½ cups shredded cheddar

¼ cup finely chopped chives

1. In a large skillet, bring about ¼ inch water to boil. Add cauliflower, cover pan, and steam until tender, about 4 minutes. Drain and let cool while you prep other ingredients.

2. In a large skillet over medium heat, cook bacon until crispy, about 3 minutes per side. Transfer to a paper towel–lined plate to drain, then chop.

3. In a large bowl, whisk together sour cream, mayonnaise, lemon juice, and garlic powder. Add cauliflower and toss gently. Season with salt and pepper, then fold in bacon, cheddar, and chives. Serve warm or at room temperature.

SNACKS

SPINACH ARTICHOKE ZUCCHINI BITES

MAKES 2 DOZEN • TOTAL TIME: 30 MIN

Spinach artichoke dip is our love language, so we're always seeking out new ways to eat it. Topping it on zucchini coins and baking until golden is the perfect anytime snack (or dinner, depending on who you ask).

---

4 ounces cream cheese, softened

⅔ cup shredded mozzarella

¼ cup freshly grated Parmesan

½ cup canned artichoke hearts, drained and chopped

½ cup frozen spinach, thawed and drained

2 tablespoons sour cream

2 cloves garlic, minced

Pinch crushed red pepper flakes

Kosher salt

Freshly ground black pepper

3 medium zucchini, cut into ½-inch rounds

---

1. Preheat oven to 400° and line a large baking sheet with parchment paper. In a medium bowl, combine cream cheese, mozzarella, Parmesan, artichokes, spinach, sour cream, garlic, and crushed red pepper. Season with salt and pepper.

2. Spread about a tablespoon of cream cheese mixture on top of each zucchini coin.

3. Bake until zucchini is tender and cheese is melty, 15 minutes. For more color, broil on high, 1 to 2 minutes.

ROASTED CHICKPEAS

SERVES 4 • TOTAL TIME: 50 MIN

New favorite snack alert! Who knew you could transform a can of chickpeas into this addictively crunchy 3 PM fix?! We love this spice blend of cumin, chili powder, and oregano, but you can also make them sweet by tossing with some brown sugar and cinnamon.

---

1 (15-ounce) can chickpeas, drained and rinsed

1 tablespoon vegetable oil

½ teaspoon kosher salt

1 teaspoon cumin

1 teaspoon chili powder

½ teaspoon dried oregano

1. Preheat oven to 350°. Pour chickpeas onto baking sheet in an even layer.

2. When oven is heated, place chickpeas in oven until completely dry, 8 to 10 minutes.

3. Remove chickpeas from oven and toss with oil and salt. Return to oven and bake until golden brown, dry, and crispy, 33 to 35 minutes, tossing halfway through.

4. Combine chickpeas and seasonings on sheet tray and toss to combine. Spread into an even layer and let cool completely.

5. To store, place in a resealable bag or air-tight container, with the bag slightly open or lid ajar to maintain crispness.

WATERMELON FRUIT ROLL-UPS

SERVES 6 · TOTAL TIME: 3 HR 15 MIN

Making fruit leather at home only sounds shi-shi—it just requires some patience. The fruit has to bake in a very low oven for three hours until it's totally dried out, sticky, and rollable. We add just a little sugar and a hefty amount of lime juice for a citrusy kick.

Cooking spray

8 cups cubed watermelon

½ cup granulated sugar

Juice of 1 lime

1. Preheat oven to 170° and line a quarter sheet pan with parchment paper. Lightly grease with cooking spray. In a blender, blend watermelon until smooth.

2. Over a fine mesh strainer lined with cheesecloth (or paper towels), drain almost all liquid from watermelon puree until you have about 2 cups watermelon solids. (Save juice for another use!)

3. In a medium bowl, whisk together watermelon solids, sugar, and lime juice.

4. Divide mixture between prepared baking sheets, spreading with an offset spatula to make smooth even layers. Bake until dried out and no longer sticky, 3 to 4 hours.

5. Using scissors, cut leather into vertical strips and roll up.

CREAMY AVOCADO DIP

SERVES 4 • TOTAL TIME: 5 MIN

Next time you're scanning the fridge hangry wondering what you can throw together in five minutes flat, remember this guac–ish dip. Greek yogurt adds protein and a creamy texture. Perfect with crudité.

2 ripe avocados

½ cup plain Greek yogurt

2 cloves garlic, minced

Juice of 1 lime

Kosher salt

Freshly ground black pepper

Pita or tortilla chips and vegetable sticks, for serving

1. In a medium bowl, mash avocados with a fork.

2. Stir in yogurt, garlic, and lime juice and season generously with salt and pepper.

3. Serve with chips and vegetables.

ANTIPASTO BITES

MAKES 20 • TOTAL TIME: 15 MIN

Cheese tortellini on a stick?! Here for it. Tossing the mozzarella balls in olive oil, Italian seasoning, and red pepper flakes is a party trick to remember. Not a fan of olives? We love these with pepperoncini, too.

---

1 tablespoon plus ½ cup extra-virgin olive oil, divided

9 ounces fresh cheese tortellini

Kosher salt

Freshly ground black pepper

2 tablespoons balsamic vinegar

8 ounces mozzarella balls (such as Ciliegine)

½ teaspoon Italian seasoning

¼ teaspoon red pepper flakes

4 ounces sliced salami

¼ pound roasted red peppers, chopped into bite-sized pieces

1 bunch fresh basil

14 ounces artichoke hearts, drained and chopped into bite-sized pieces

¼ pound green olives

1. In a large pot of boiling water, add 1 tablespoon oil. Cook tortellini according to package instructions until al dente. Drain and transfer to large bowl.

2. Season cooked tortellini with salt and pepper. Add balsamic vinegar and ¼ cup olive oil and mix to combine. Set aside.

3. Marinate mozzarella: In a small bowl, add mozzarella balls, Italian seasoning, red pepper flakes, and remaining ¼ cup olive oil. Mix to combine and set aside.

4. Assemble skewers by layering one piece each mozzarella, salami, roasted red pepper, tortellini, basil, artichoke heart, and green olives.

BACON PARM CRACKERS

SERVES 6 • TOTAL TIME: 1 HR

The first time we tried this recipe, we were skeptical: bacon wrapped around...crackers?! One bite and we immediately understood: The crackers, Parmesan, and bacon meld into one savory, dreamy bite.

---

1 package bacon strips, cut in half
32 Club Crackers
½ cup freshly grated Parmesan
Freshly ground black pepper
Ranch dressing, for dipping

1. Preheat oven to 350° and line a large baking sheet with parchment paper.

2. Arrange crackers on baking sheet and sprinkle with Parmesan. Tightly wrap each cracker with bacon and place seam-side down, then top with more Parmesan.

3. Bake until bacon is cooked through and bites are crispy, 45 to 50 minutes.

4. Season with pepper and serve with ranch for dipping.

PIZZA-STUFFED MUSHROOMS

MAKES 20 · TOTAL TIME: 25 MIN

Mushrooms might not be the vegetable that typically gets all the attention, but when you turn them into pizza we're listening. This is definitely the easiest way to stuff a 'shroom—no filling to mix or stems to sauté.

---

20 baby mushrooms

2 tablespoons butter

2 cloves garlic, minced

⅓ cup bread crumbs

Kosher salt

Freshly ground black pepper

¼ cup freshly grated Parmesan

¼ cup marinara sauce

1 cup low-moisture shredded mozzarella

½ cup mini pepperoni

Torn basil, for garnish

---

1. Preheat oven to 400°. Remove stems from mushrooms and roughly chop stems. Place mushroom caps on baking sheet.

2. In a large ovenproof skillet, over medium heat, melt butter. Add chopped mushrooms stems and cook until most of the moisture is out, 5 minutes. Add garlic and cook until fragrant, 1 minute then add bread crumbs and let toast slightly, 3 minutes. Season with salt and pepper. Remove from heat and let cool slightly. Wipe skillet clean.

3. In a large bowl mix together mushroom stem mixture, Parmesan, and marinara. Season with salt and pepper. Fill mushroom caps with filling and place in skillet, about 1 inch apart. Sprinkle tops with mozzarella and mini pepperoni.

4. Bake until mushrooms are soft and the tops are golden, 20 minutes.

5. Garnish with basil before serving.

GREEK

Dill + kalamata olives + feta

EVERYTHING BAGEL

Cream cheese + smoked salmon + poppy seeds

PIMENTO CHEESE

Pimiento peppers + cheddar

BLT

Bacon + lettuce + tomato

BUFFALO

Blue cheese + hot sauce

GUACAMOLE

Lime juice + avocado

JALAPEÑO POPPER

Cheddar + jalapeño + cream cheese

BACON JALAPEÑO

Bacon + jalapeño + scallions

DILL PICKLE

Dill pickles + Old Bay

DEVILED EGG, 9 WAYS

MAKES 12 • TOTAL TIME: 40 MIN

Best. Snack. Ever. Crack into these delicious ways to upgrade the classic finger food.

---

6 large eggs

¼ cup mayonnaise

1 teaspoon hot sauce

1 teaspoon Dijon mustard

Kosher salt

Freshly ground black pepper

Desired toppings, see left page

1. Place eggs in a large saucepan and cover with cold water. Set pan over medium–high heat and bring water to a boil. Turn off heat, cover pan with a lid, and let sit for 11 minutes. Drain, rinse eggs under cold water, and peel.

2. Halve eggs lengthwise and scoop out yolks into a medium bowl. Add mayonnaise, hot sauce, and Dijon mustard to bowl, then mash yolks with the back of a fork and stir until mixture is smooth. Season with salt and pepper.

3. Spoon mixture into each egg. Top as desired.

CARAMEL APPLE NACHOS

SERVES 6 • TOTAL TIME: 15 MIN

Where have apple nachos been all our life?! Assembling this dessert–y snack might be even more fun than eating it. Put out a spread of all your toppings—any kind of chocolate, caramel or peanut butter, pretzels, chopped candy bars, nuts—and let things get messy.

---

4 Granny Smith apples, cored and thinly sliced

1 cup white chocolate chips, melted

¾ cup caramel, warmed

1 cup chopped pretzels

2 Heath bars, broken into pieces

1. On a large plate, arrange apple slices on top of one another.

2. Drizzle with half the white chocolate and caramel, then top with pretzels and Heath bars.

3. Drizzle with remaining white chocolate and caramel.

4. Serve immediately.

EVERYTHING BAGEL POPCORN

SERVES 4 • TOTAL TIME: 10 MIN

An instant way to make pretty much anything taste 1,000 times better? Everything bagel seasoning. We blend up our own here with sesame and poppy seeds, minced onion, garlic powder, and salt, but most grocery stores sell it in jars now if you want a shortcut.

---

1 bag light popcorn
2 tablespoons butter, melted
2 tablespoons sesame seeds
1 tablespoon poppy seeds
1 tablespoon dried minced onion
1 teaspoon garlic powder
1 teaspoon kosher salt

1. Pop the popcorn according to the package's instructions.

2. Place the popcorn in a gallon-sized resealable bag and add remaining ingredients. Seal and shake to coat, then serve.

SALAMI CHIPS

SERVES 4 · TOTAL TIME: 30 MIN

Prepare to have your mind blown: Baking up plain slices of salami—nothing on them at all—in the oven turns them into crispy, salty pieces of gold. These are perfect on their own, but we always love a good dipping sauce.

½ **pound sliced salami, about ⅛ inch thick**

½ **cup mayonnaise**

2 tablespoons red wine vinegar

1 tablespoon parsley, finely chopped

2 teaspoons Dijon mustard

1 teaspoon dried oregano

Kosher salt

Freshly ground black pepper

---

1. Preheat oven to 325° and line a medium baking sheet with parchment paper. Place salami in a single layer on baking sheet and bake until crisp, 20 to 25 minutes.

2. Meanwhile, make sauce: In a medium bowl, combine remaining ingredients. Whisk until smooth.

3. Serve salami chips with sauce on side.

PASTA CHIPS

SERVES 6 · TOTAL TIME: 30 MIN

The lovechild of two of our favorite food groups.
Boiling the bowties until they're al dente ensures
the chips keep a nice chew after you fry them up.
Whatever your favorite jarred sauce (marinara, vodka,
or pesto) works as a dunker.

---

1 pound bowtie pasta

Vegetable oil, for frying

**½ cup freshly grated
Parmesan**

**1 teaspoon Italian
seasoning**

1 teaspoon garlic powder

Kosher salt

**Freshly ground black
pepper**

Marinara, for serving

1. In a large pot of salted boiling
water, cook pasta until al dente,
about 8 minutes. Drain pasta.

2. In a large, deep skillet, pour
about ½ inch vegetable oil and
heat over medium heat. When oil
is shimmering, add about 1 cup
al dente pasta in a single layer.
Cook until golden and crispy,
about 2 minutes per side. Drain
on paper towels, then season
immediately with Parmesan,
Italian seasoning, garlic powder,
salt, and pepper.

3. Repeat, working in batches,
with the rest of the pasta.

4. Serve with warm marinara.

MORE FROM DELISH

You'll find everything you could possibly want in one of our cookbooks—whether it's a weeknight chicken dinner, an easy Instant Pot side, an epic air fryer appetizer, or an over-the-top dessert. We've got it all.

KETO FOR CARB LOVERS
100+ Amazing Low-Carb, High-Fat Recipes

PARTY IN AN AIR FRYER
75+ Guilt-Free Air Fryer Recipes

PARTY IN AN INSTANT POT®
75+ Crazy Simple Recipes Made in Your Multi Cooker

KETO FOR DESSERT LOVERS
75+ Low-Carb, High-Fat Sweets

INSANELY EASY CHICKEN DINNERS
90+ Delicious Weeknight Dinners

INSANELY EASY CASSEROLES
80+ Easy & Comforting Casseroles

ULTIMATE COCKTAILS
100+ Fun & Delicious
Cocktail Recipes

INSANE SWEETS
100+ Cookies, Bars,
Bites & Treats

**EAT LIKE EVERY DAY'S
THE WEEKEND**
275+ Amazing Recipe Ideas!

KETO STARTER GUIDE
Essential Recipes, Tips &
Tricks For Keto Beginners

CHECK THEM OUT AT:

Store.Delish.com and Amazon